The Final Five

The Ultimate UNOFFICIAL Guide

The Final Five

The *Ultimate* UNOFFICIAL Guide

BY Emily **Pullman**

GymnStars Volume 11

Creative Media Publishing

CREATIVE MEDIA, INC.
PO Box 6270
Whittier, California 90609-6270
United States of America

Book & cover design by Joseph Dzidrums

www.creativemedia.net

First Edition: November 2016

LCCN: On File
ISBN 978-1-938438-97-4
eISBN: 978-1-938438-98-1

To every past, present, and future olympian

TABLE OF CONTENTS

"No matter what, [the Final Five] are always looking out for each other and have each other's back. We're here to support each other." - Simone Biles

Many sports fans regard the *Final Five* as America's greatest women's gymnastics team ever. The beloved quintet dominated the 2016 Rio Olympics, winning the team competition by a whopping 8+ points. They also scored eight individual gold medals: three gold, four silver, and one bronze.

The Final Five
Ricardo Bufolin

So, which gymnasts comprise the Final Five? How did they get their iconic name? What were their lives like before and after their Olympic triumphs?

Read on for the answers. *The Final Five: The Ultimate Unofficial Guide* profiles the most successful American gymnastics team ever.

Sisterhood
Ricardo Bufolin

The Final Five at the MTV VMAs

Aaron J Thornton / PR Photos

*"I'm not the next
Usain Bolt or Michael Phelps.
I'm the first Simone Biles."*

Simone Arianne Biles was born on March 14, 1997, in Columbus, Ohio. At the time of her birth, two phenoms were taking their respective sports by storm. Twenty-one-year-old Tiger Woods was weeks away from winning his first major championship. Meanwhile, in a few days' time, fourteen-year-old ice skater Tara Lipinski would capture the world figure skating championship. So, it seemed fitting that a tiny burst of energy named Simone entered the world that year. Like the aforementioned athletes, she would one day turn her sport – gymnastics – upside down.

At a young age, Simone and her younger sister, Adria, left the Buckeye State behind. They moved to Houston, Texas, to live with their grandparents, who formally adopted them. Meanwhile, her two brothers remained in Ohio with their biological mother.

When Simone was six years old, she visited

a gym with her daycare class. The youngster's eye lit up with excitement at the discovery of the thrilling sport. She stood on the sidelines, closely watching the gymnasts perform different skills.

"While there, I imitated the other gymnasts, and Coach Ronnie noticed," Simone later recalled. "The gym sent home a letter requesting that I join tumbling or gymnastics."

Coach Ronnie thought fellow instructor Aimee Boorman would work well with the new gymnast. She was correct. The two clicked immediately, and Simone acquired several gymnastics skills at lightning speed.

Simone celebrates a great routine.
Ricardo Bufolin

Simon loved gymnastics so much, she sometimes forgot to leave the tricks at the gym. The excited child often practiced skills at home using the family sofa for soft landings! Eventually, the Biles bought a trampoline so their daughter could jump to her heart's content without ruining any furniture!

Simone watched televised gymnastics at every opportunity. The seven-year-old marveled when American Carly Patterson won the all-around gold medal at the 2004 Athens Olympics. She admired the Texan's explosive gymnastics and wanted to be like her.

As the years passed, Simone gained new skills and improved her overall gymnastics. A strong competitor, she accumulated a large medal collection. By the age of 14, the teenager was one of America's best junior gymnasts.

In the fall of 2012, Simone entered high school. That same year she started home schooling. The new educational structure allowed her schedule more flexibility for the pursuit of gymnastics.

Game Face
Ricardo Bufolin

Despite being in a non-traditional school environment, Simone was expected to maintain good grades, which she did. Her favorite class was history. However, she didn't like math, especially Algebra.

In the summer of 2012, the nation's top gymnasts battled for a spot on the U.S. Olympic team. Because Simone was too young to compete at the competition, she remained a junior-level gymnast for another year. At the USA Gymnastics National Championships, she won the all-around bronze medal and took gold on the vault.

When Simone watched the 2012 Olympics on television that summer. Excitement rippled through her. It felt thrilling to watch her friends competing for Team USA. In the end, the United States girls' gymnastics team, dubbed the *Fierce Five*, won team gold and scored four individual medals.

The following year, Simone moved to the senior level. Initially, the young gymnast delivered uneven results. She often competed well at one competition but struggled at the next event. Hoping to improve her consistency, she began working with a sports psychologist. Her doctor taught her ways to feel more relaxed and confident in competition.

Simone tested her new competitive approach at the 2013 USA Gymnastics National Championships in Hartford, Connecticut. Many expected Fierce Five member Kyla Ross to win the individual all-around title, but a determined Texan had other plans. The newly-minted senior delivered spellbinding routines that propelled her to the national title. Simone Biles became the number one gymnast in America!

WORLD 2013
CHAMPIONSHIPS
ARTISTIC GYMNASTICS
30/09 - 06/10 ANTWERP
www.antwerpgymnastics2013.com

Antwerp, Belgium, hosted the 2013 World Gymnastics Championships. Simone arrived at her first worlds as America's top gymnast. In the individual all-around event, the newly inspired athlete soundly defeated Kyla Ross by nearly a full point to become world champion!

Remarkably, Simone also qualified for all four individual event finals. She was the first American female gymnast to accomplish the feat since Shannon Miller in 1991. In the end, Simone picked up three more individual medals: floor gold, vault silver, and a bronze on the balance beam.

Simone's confidence skyrocketed after her first successful senior season. The teenager ce-

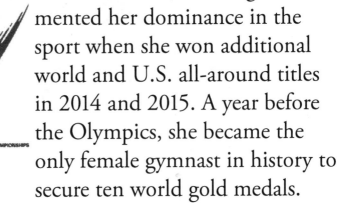

45ᵗʰ FIG ARTISTIC GYMNASTICS WORLD CHAMPIONSHIPS
NANNING(CHN)

mented her dominance in the sport when she won additional world and U.S. all-around titles in 2014 and 2015. A year before the Olympics, she became the only female gymnast in history to secure ten world gold medals.

In the summer of 2016, Simone's childhood dream came true. She arrived in Rio to compete at the Olympics. An overwhelming favorite to win several medals, the nineteen-year-old tried to ignore the bright spotlight shining on her and concentrated on performing to her best ability!

Simone kicked off her Olympic experience in the team event. Four other gifted athletes comprised the USA's women's gymnastics squad: Gabby Douglas, Laurie Hernandez, Madison Kocian, and Aly Raisman. All the women delivered strong routines on both nights of competition. In the end, USA won the team title by a whopping 8 points over Russia, the silver medalists. Meanwhile, China placed third.

Simone competes in Rio.
Ricardo Bufolin

Simone competed next in the individual all-around, gymnastics' most prestigious title. Wearing a sparkly red, white, and blue leotard, Simone performed brilliantly in all four phases of the event. She closed her quest for gold with an exhilarating floor exercise routine that propelled her to victory.

Simone felt delighted when her teammate and good friend, Aly Raisman, snatched the silver medal. The two girls shared a warm hug after learning of their one-two finish. The crowd cheered even louder when they shared a joint curtain call.

All-around Podium
Ricardo Bufolin

Simone wins the Olympic all-around event.
Ricardo Bufolin

"Every emotion hit me at once," Simone remarked. "Everything was going through my head. I had finally done it, and when that hits you, you can't really stop the emotions."

Individual apparatus events would complete the Olympic competition. Simone qualified for every final except the uneven bars. Ultimately, she collected three more medals: vault gold, floor gold, and balance beam bronze. In all, Simone ended her Rio experience with five medals: four gold and one bronze.

Simone is deep in concentration.
Ricardo Bufolin

Simone's amazing Rio experience wasn't over yet, though. One afternoon, NBC's *Today Show* surprised Simone by introducing the gymnast to her celebrity crush, Zac Efron. The smitten teenager felt thrilled to meet her favorite actor. The two shared a hug and enjoyed a brief chat.

Simone received another huge surprise near the end of the Rio Games. Team USA selected her to carry the American flag at the event's closing ceremonies. The enormous honor thrilled her.

Simone with the President and First Lady
The White House

"I'm very excited, and I can't wait for my team to be with me so I can do that," she stated.

Following the Olympics, the Final Five flew to New York to appear on *The Tonight Show Starring Jimmy Fallon*. The women also toured the Empire State Building, presented at the *MTV Video Music Awards*, and caught a performance of the Broadway musical *Hamilton*. Individually, Simone also appeared on *Ellen* and visited the *Pretty Little Liars* set!

As 2016 neared its end, Simone announced that she would take a year break from competition. The youngster had trained tirelessly for years and needed rest. Although the sports world would miss the bright star, they understood her decision. If anyone deserved a breather, it was Simone Biles.

Simone poses on the red carpet.
PR Photos

SIMONE BILES LINKS

FACEBOOK
facebook.com/simonebiles

TWITTER
twitter.com/Simone_Biles

INSTAGRAM
instagram.com/simonebiles

GKEIITE SIMONE BILES LEOTARDS
gkelite.com/gymnastics-shopby-simonebilesleotards

USA GYMNASTICS PROFILE
usagym.org/pages/athletes/athleteListDetail.html?id=164887

SIMONE'S FAVORITES

FOOD
Pepperoni Pizza

COLOR
Purple

TV SHOW
Pretty Little Liars

VACATION SPOT
Belize

SCHOOL SUBJECT
History

DOG BREED
German Shepherd

WINTER SPORT
Snowboarding

EVENT
Floor

GYMNAST
Alicia Sacramone

BOOK
The Hunger Games series

MOVIE
Vacation, Mean Girls

SIMONE'S COMPETITIVE RECORD HIGHLIGHTS

2016 OLYMPIC GAMES

Team – 1

All-Around – 1

Vault -1

Floor Exercise – 1

Balance Beam – 2

2016 OLYMPIC TRIALS

All-Around -1

2016 US CHAMPIONSHIPS

All-Around – 1

2015 WORLD CHAMPIONSHIPS

Team – 1

All-Around – 1

Floor Exercise – 1

Balance Beam – 1

Vault -3

2015 US CHAMPIONSHIPS

All-Around – 1

2014 WORLD CHAMPIONSHIPS

Team – 1

All-Around – 1

Floor Exercise – 1

Balance Beam – 1

Vault – 2

2014 US CHAMPIONSHIPS

All-Around – 1

2013 WORLD CHAMPIONSHIPS

All-Around – 1

Floor Exercise – 1

Vault – 2

Balance Beam – 3

2013 US CHAMPIONSHIPS

All-Around – 1

"If you push through the hard days, then you can get through anything."

When Gabby Douglas stepped onto the competitive floor at the Rio Games, she became the first female all-around champion since Romania's Nadia Comaneci to appear at a second Olympics. She'd already won two Olympic titles in 2012. Could she win another gold medal?

Gabrielle Christina Victoria Douglas was born on December 31, 1995, in Virginia Beach, Virginia. The New Year's Day baby was the youngest of four children. She had three older siblings: Johnathan, Joyelle, and Arielle.

Virginia Beach, Virginia

Gabby and her mom, Natalie Hawkins

Seth El / PR Photos

Arielle was the first family member to take gymnastics lessons. Whenever the older sister returned home from class, she taught that day's skills to Gabby, who picked up the moves flawlessly. Eventually, the younger sister also began taking gymnastics classes.

Gabby fell in love with the sport quickly. On lesson days, the youngster could scarcely contain her excitement. She loved every gymnastics apparatus: balance beam, floor, and vault. However, the tiny girl particularly adored the uneven bars. She flew so high during release moves that sometimes onlookers gasped in awe. How could someone so small fly so high? Years later, Gabby earned the nickname *The Flying Squirrel*, inspired by the amazing height she achieved.

Gabby always followed gymnastics on television, too. In the summer of 2008, she watched the Beijing Olympic Games. Her favorite gymnast, Iowa's Shawn Johnson, won one gold and three silver Olympic medals under the guidance of her longtime coach, Liang Chow.

Gabby wanted to compete at the Olympics, too. She would love to compete on gymnastics' biggest stage. What an honor it would be to represent the United States at the Olympics.

At the 2010 USA Gymnastics National Championships, Gabby finished fourth in the junior all-around competition. It was a solid finish, but the young gymnast needed to be better if she wanted to make the next Olympic team. She begged her reluctant mother to let her move to Iowa to train with Liang Chow. Eventually, her mom agreed, although she hated seeing her daughter leave.

Chow placed Gabby in a home with a terrific host family. The Partons were a large, loving household that accepted Gabby into their lives with open arms. The family's kindness and generosity helped curb the gymnast's ongoing homesickness.

Despite missing her family, Gabby felt confident in her decision to train away from home. Since Coach Chow had guided her hero, Shawn Johnson, to Olympic gold, she hoped he could do the same for her. Of course, the gymnast would have to work harder than ever.

Gabby competes in Rio.
Ricardo Bufolin

Gabby's diligent work paid off when she made the world team the following year. The youngest competitor on the squad, the fifteen-year-old did not act intimidated at her first world championships. Instead, she delivered a solid uneven bars routine in the team competition, helping to propel the United States to the gold medal.

The following season, Gabby felt more confident than ever. Under Chow's tutelage, she had upgraded skills on every apparatus. The teen-ager couldn't wait to compete and show off her improvements.

Gabby appears on The Tonight Show.
NBC

Ultimately, Gabby won second place at the USA Gymnastics National Championships. A few weeks later, she claimed first place at Olympic Trials and officially earned a trip to the 2012 London Olympics! In the end, five supremely talented ladies comprised Team USA: Gabby, Jordyn Wieber, Aly Raisman, McKayla Maroney, and Kyla Ross.

Before the London Games, sports pundits predicted that the United States women would easily win the gymnastics team event. Images of all five girls were splashed everywhere. The squad even made the cover of *Sports Illustrated Magazine*.

Gabby eyes the beam.
Ricardo Bufolin

Once in London, the American women did not disappoint. They took team gold in commanding fashion, winning the competition by over five points. Upon discovering they had won, the five girls embraced one another before shouting, "USA!"

Gabby's Olympic experience resumed with the all-around event. The sixteen-year-old had three main challengers for the gold medal: Russians Aliya Mustafina and Viktoria Komova, and American teammate Aly Raisman. In the end, Gabby executed four flawless routines and earned the victory! She also became the first African-American gymnast to win Olympic all-around gold.

Gabby became an international star following the Olympics. She endorsed commercial products, appeared on television talk shows, and even starred on a reality series. Lifetime Television also aired a movie based on her life!

However, after a few years away from the sport, Gabby missed gymnastics. She craved another Olympic experience. So, the teenager announced a return to the sport that made her a star.

Gabby poses with her Teen Choice Award.
Andrew Evans / PR Photos

The Gabby Douglas Barbie
Mattel

In the beginning of 2015, Gabby officially returned to competitive gymnastics. At the national championships, she finished a respectable fourth in the all-around behind the sport's newest sensation, Simone Biles. Several months later, the Olympic champion won her first individual world medal by placing second behind Simone at the 2015 World Gymnastics Championships.

The following season, Gabby began working with coach Christian Gallardo at Buckeye Gymnastics in Ohio. She won all-around titles at City of Jesolo and the American Cup.

Golden Again!
Ricardo Bufolin

Although the twenty-year-old struggled slightly at the 2016 Olympic Trials, she still made the Rio team.

"I'm really excited to go back and clean up details, add a few extra tenths (of a point) here and there, and really just push myself," she remarked. "I'm really excited."

At the Rio Olympics, Gabby performed well on both days of team competition. Not surprisingly, she particularly shined on the uneven bars. The popular gymnast's strong contributions helped Team USA to a gold medal finish.

A rule limits two athletes per county to compete in the individual all-around competition. Although Gabby placed third in the team all-around, her teammates, Simone and Aly, finished 1-2, respectively. Therefore, Gabby was left on the sidelines and could not defend her all-around title.

The twenty-year-old had plenty to be proud of, though. She now owned three Olympic gold medals. Plus, she had become the first women's Olympic all-around champion in 36 years to compete at a second Olympics.

Following the Rio Olympics, Gabby made several media appearances and joined the *Kellogg's Tour of Gymnastics Champions.* When she performed every night, young girls cheered loudly for her, delighted to see their idol in person. There was no doubt about it. Gabby wasn't just one of gymnastics' biggest stars, she was a sports icon.

Gabby smiles at the 2014 Kid's Choice Awards.
Andrew Evans / PR Photos

GABBY DOUGLAS LINKS

FACEBOOK
facebook.com/GabrielleDouglasUSA

TWITTER
twitter.com/gabrielledoug

INSTAGRAM
instagram.com/gabbycvdouglas

OFFICIAL WEBSITE
gabrielledouglas.com

GK ELITE GABBY DOUGLAS LEOTARDS
gkelite.com/Gymnastics-Shopby-GabrielleDouglasLeotards

GABBY'S FAVORITES

FOOD
Italian, Mexican

SCHOOL SUBJECT
English

VACATION SPOT
Bora Bora

SPORTS TEAM
Los Angeles Lakers

BAND
One Direction

COLOR
Yellow

OTHER SPORT
Track and Field

ATHLETES
LeBron James and Kobe Bryant

HOBBY
Knitting

TELEVISION SHOW
The Vampire Diaries

MOVIE
Hunger Games: Catching Fire

FAVORITE SWEET
Chocolate

PRE-COMPETITION RITUAL
Meditating

GABBY'S COMPETITIVE RECORD HIGHLIGHTS

2016 OLYMPIC GAMES
Team – 1

2015 WORLD CHAMPIONSHIPS
Team – 1
All-Around – 2

2012 OLYMPIC GAMES
Team - 1
All-Around – 1

2012 OLYMPIC TRIALS
All-Around – 1

2012 US CHAMPIONSHIPS
All-Around – 2

2011 WORLD CHAMPIONSHIPS
Team – 1

*"I'm living the dream
and the path that I've wanted
to take for so long that
I should just enjoy the ride."*

Laurie Hernandez was competing at the most stressful competition of her life: the 2016 Rio Olympics. You'd never have known it by her playful demeanor, though. The 16-year-old smiled, winked, and flirted with the crowd and judges, all while contending for a gold medal.

In the team event final, Laurie nearly skipped onto the blue mat to perform her floor-exercise routine. She assumed her start position by raising her hands above her head. When her music began, the confident gymnast smiled brightly and winked at the judges. It was a rare display of personality in a sport often packed with stoic looking contenders.

Laurie's confidence and spirited personality were likely rooted in experience. She had been a gymnast for more than 2/3 of her life. Gymnastics had been her home since she was five. By age seven, she had vowed to compete at the Olympics one day.

Lauren Zoe Hernandez was born on June 9, 2000, in New Brunswick, New Jersey. She was the youngest child of Anthony, a county clerk for the New York City Supreme Court, and Wanda, an elementary school social worker. She also had a sister named Jelysa and a brother, Marcus.

Aerial view of New Jersey, Laurie's home state

At age three, Laurie's parents enrolled her in ballet lessons. When the little girl refused to go to her first class, her parents bribed her with sugar cookies. Not surprisingly, their daughter grew restless with classical dance, craving a faster-paced activity.

One day Laurie watched a televised gymnastics competition. The sports merger of acrobatics and music mesmerized her. She begged her mother and father to let her try the sport, and they agreed.

Laurie began taking lessons under Carly Haney's tutelage. The youngster flourished in the recreational class. Within six weeks of starting classes, Laurie learned a cartwheel and a split.

Recognizing Laurie's phenomenal talent, Carly sent the youngster to train with her sister, Maggie. The two hit it off instantly.

"Laurie is like my first born," Margaret told *The Guardian*. "She sleeps over at my house, she has dinner with my family, we watch movies in my bed, and I tuck her in at night. My own daughter calls Laurie her sister."

Laurie felt equally fond of Maggie. She always credited her coach with a huge part of her success. After all, she learned nearly every gymnastics skill from her.

"I can't see myself with anybody else," Laurie remarked. "I don't think I would have come this far with anybody else."

The talented athlete can also thank Maggie's family for her nickname, *Lolo*. When her coach's daughter could not pronounce Laurie, she said Lolo instead, and the name stuck.

Incidentally, Laurie wasn't the only Hernandez child blessed with an athletic gift. Marcus ran on his school's track and field team. Meanwhile, Jelysa earned a black belt in karate.

On a typical training day, Laurie rose at 7 a.m. and ate a healthy breakfast, usually oatmeal and fruit. By 8:30, she was training at the gym, remaining there for five to six hours. When the teenager returned home, she finished her homework, ate dinner, relaxed, and went to bed.

Laurie didn't mind the strict regime. A rigid routine came naturally to her. Her mom served in the Army Reserve.

"[My mom] taught me the importance of following rules, finishing what I start, never giving up, leadership skills, teamwork, staying positive, motivated, and how to pack the military way when I'm traveling!" Laurie told *NBCOlympics.com.*

Laurie flashes her winning style.
Ricardo Bufolin

Although Laurie loved gymnastics, she made time to partake in a variety of enjoyable activities. An avid reader, she often became absorbed in good books. When the teenager wanted a more physical pastime, she learned different dance moves by watching *YouTube* clips. Sometimes she simply baked a delicious dessert.

When looking for entertainment, Laurie grabbed a bowl of frozen yogurt and planted herself in front of the television. Usually, she watched a favorite show, like *Dancing with the Stars*, *The Voice*, or *Law and Order*.

A film buff, Laurie always welcomed a good movie. *Stars Wars* and *Return of the Jedi* were her favorite flicks. Naturally, she felt thrilled when the film franchise's long-awaited sequel *The Force Awakens* premiered in movie theaters.

"I love *Star Wars* because I have seen the first six movies when I was younger, she told *NBCOlympics. com.* "[*The Force Awakens*] was amazing, especially how the movie lived up to my expectations."

Laurie poses for the camera.
PR Photos

A musical person, Laurie liked listening to inspirational music before competitions. Her favorite tunes included: "Can't Sleep" by Pentatonix, Martin Garrix's "Don't Look Down," "Chemicals" by Tiësto, Diplo's "Be Right There," and Kelly Clarkson songs.

Although Laurie welcomed the many distractions, gymnastics always sat in the forefront of her thoughts. Ultimately, 2015 was Laurie's breakout season. She earned the junior all-around title at the USA Gymnastics National Championships. The talented phenom followed up the victory with wins at City of Jesolo Trophy and the U.S. Classic.

Since 2016 was an Olympic year, Laurie wanted to make the Rio team. To do so, she needed to prove her consistency, and she did. At nationals, she placed third in four events: all-around, balance beam, floor exercise, and uneven bars. Her steady performances impressed the right people.

"She didn't feel intimidated, and she did what she was prepared for," raved Martha Karolyi, the U.S. national team coordinator.

Leaping through the floor routine
Ricardo Bufolin

"That's exactly what you look for, to see if she can handle the pressure and if she feels comfortable with that setting."

Having impressed at nationals, Laurie needed a similar finish at Olympic trials to solidify a spot on the team. She did even better than at nationals, finishing second in the all-around. When officials announced the Olympic team, Laurie's name was called!

"Wow. That's all I can really say," she gushed. "Looking back at this little girl watching the Olympics on her phone, I would never think I'd be here right now."

Laurie's outgoing personality sparkled at the Rio Olympics. Sports fans loved the teenager with magnificent hair and a dazzling smile. Thanks to her outgoing, expressive personality, she earned the nickname, *The Human Emoji*.

"I want to make sure I always show off my smile and have a positive attitude the whole time, whether it's during a performance, practice, or doing an interview," Laurie confided to *TheGuardian.com*.

Laurie flashes her radiant smile.
PRN / PR Photos

Laurie also gained attention for being the first U.S.-born Hispanic female gymnast on America's Olympic squad since Tracee Talavera in 1984. The second-generation Puerto Rican felt proud of her heritage.

"I feel I could be a role model to other Hispanic gymnasts interested in the sport," she remarked. "I also want them to understand the importance of being focused, determined, and not giving up, despite all the struggles."

Ultimately, Laurie had a great Olympic experience. She made two podium appearances in Rio, a team gold with the Final Five and a silver medal on the balance beam.

By the time the final piece of confetti fell at the closing ceremonies, she was already one of the Olympics' most high profile personalities. Laurie enjoyed her newfound celebrity status. She appeared on several talk shows, toured with *Kellogg's Tour of Gymnastics Champions*, and earned a Proctor and Gamble deal to promote Crest.

Laurie on Dancing with the Stars

ABC

Perhaps Laurie's most exciting post-Olympic experience? She competed on the smash hit TV series *Dancing with the Stars*. Paired with professional dancer Val Chmerkovskiy, the perky Olympian became an instant fan favorite and a judges' darling. In the season's fourth week, she set a show record by earning perfect 10s from every judge! She eventually took first place in the competition.

"It felt amazing," Laurie told *Good Morning America*. "I had that same joy as I had at the Olympics. It was exciting."

Olympic gold medals, 10.0 scores, and the adoration of many fans. Laurie lived a dream life, one for which she had worked hard. Yet despite Laurie's enormous success and newfound fame, the likable sixteen-year old remained as down-to-earth and humble as ever. Her parents always kept her grounded.

"We tried to teach her the art of gratefulness," her mother once remarked.

And sports fans can attest that the quality shines brightly in Laurie Hernandez!

Laurie wins Dancing with the Stars
ABC

LAURIE HERNANDEZ LINKS

TWITTER
twitter.com/lzhernandez02

INSTAGRAM
instagram.com/lauriehernandez

FACEBOOK
facebook.com/LaurieHernandezUSA

TEAM USA PROFILE
teamusa.org/usa-gymnastics/athletes/Laurie-Hernandez

WIKIPEDIA PROFILE
en.wikipedia.org/wiki/Laurie_Hernandez

LAURIE'S FAVORITES

INDULGENCE
Bath bombs

HOBBY
Painting nails

ATHLETE
Usain Bolt

NFL TEAM
New York Giants

SECRET TALENT
Writing poetry

ACTRESS
Jennifer Lawrence

VACATION SPOT
Italy, Japan, and Mexico

TV SHOW
Friends

BOOK
The Maze Runner

MOVIE
Star Wars Trilogy

MUSIC ARTIST
Tori Kelly

LAURIE'S COMPETITIVE RECORD HIGHLIGHTS

2016 OLYMPIC GAMES
Team – 1
Balance Beam – 2

2016 OLYMPIC TRIALS
All-Around – 2

2016 US CHAMPIONSHIPS
All-Around – 3

2015 US CHAMPIONSHIPS (JUNIOR)
All-Around – 1

2015 US CLASSIC (JUNIOR)
All-Around – 1
Vault – 1
Balance Beam – 1

"If you believe in yourself more than anyone else and you have a goal in mind, you can achieve it."

On June 15, 1997, Madison Taylor Kocian was born in Dallas, Texas. She was Thomas and Cindy Kocian's first child. Later, a son, Ty, completed the family

In hindsight, Madison seemed destined for gymnastics. As a toddler, she constantly climbed out of her crib with little effort. The youngster seemed impatient to get started in the world!

When Madison turned five, her parents enrolled her in gymnastics lessons at World Olympics Gymnastics Academy (WOGA). Owned by Olympic champion Valeri Liukin, it was one of the country's top gyms. The Kocians knew that people uprooted their lives and moved across the country to train at WOGA, so they fortunate to live so close to the center.

While training at the facility, Madison witnessed gymnast Carly Patterson training for various major competitions. Eventually, the veteran gymnast made the U.S. Olympic team in 2004.

Weeks later, Carly won the esteemed all-around title at the Athens Games.

Four years later, Valeri's daughter, Nastia, also made the United States Olympic gymnastics team. While at the Beijing Games, young Liukin captured all-around gold, like Carly had. It marked the first time that two American girls from the same gym had won back-to-back Olympic titles.

Madison looked up to Nastia more than any other gymnast. She admired the Olympic champion's elegant athletics and her remarkable skills on the uneven bars. Nastia was always kind to Madison, taking her under her wing and offering advice over the years.

Besides gymnastics, Madison enjoyed other sports, too. The strong swimmer visited the pool whenever she had a chance. Mostly, though, she was a proud Texas Rangers fan and attended their baseball games whenever she could. The young gymnast often dreamed of throwing out the first pitch at the ballpark.

In 2010, Madison qualified for the USA

Gymnastics National Championships on the junior level. The twelve-year-old flew to Hartford, Connecticut, to compete against America's best gymnasts. After two days of competition, she placed an impressive 5th in the all-around behind future Olympic champions Gabby Douglas and Kyla Ross. The excited Texan also took home a bronze medal in the uneven bars final.

Three years later, Madison qualified for her senior debut at the 2013 USA Gymnastics National Championships. Unfortunately, the gymnast withdrew due to an ankle injury. She felt devastated to miss such a big event.

Dallas, Texas skyline

Madison qualified for nationals again the following year. Recovering from an injury, she competed only on the uneven bars and the balance beam. On the former event, the strong competitor scored a second-straight bronze medal.

Buoyed by her strength on the uneven bars, Madison was selected to represent Team USA at the 2014 World Gymnastics Championships in Nanning, China. As the specialist, she competed solely on the uneven bars. The seventeen-year-old's solid efforts helped the United States win gold in the team competition.

Madison competes on the uneven bars.
Ricardo Bufolin

"The memories I made with my teammates in China will last forever, and I hope I will get the opportunity again to represent the USA at worlds in 2015," the thrilled gymnast told *International Gymnast Magazine.*

Madison found even greater success in the 2015 season. At nationals, she finally captured gold on the uneven bars and placed sixth in the all-around. A few months later, she flew with Team USA to worlds and returned with gold medals in the team event and uneven bars finals.

Anytime Madison traveled to a new country, she set aside sightseeing time. The teenager wanted to take advantage of her travel opportunities by exploring her surroundings. She especially loved visiting different churches since faith was an important part of her life.

When the 2016 Olympic year began, Madison felt determined to earn a spot on the Rio squad. An ankle injury hampered the early part of her season, but she rebounded later to win a silver medal on bars at nationals and the U.S. Classic.

Madison runs through her floor routine.
Ricardo Bufolin

In early July, Madison arrived in San Jose, California, to compete at the Olympic Trials. Delivering strong performances, she won the uneven bars event and placed 8th in the all-around competition.

After the trials had ended, Madison waited backstage to find out if she had made the Rio team. National Team Coordinator Marta Karolyi and other committee members debated for several minutes before they reached a decision. In the end, they selected Madison and four other strong competitors to the team!

The Final Five models their Kellogg's cereal boxes
Kellogg's

"When my name was announced, I instantly broke into tears just because you think of all the hard work and the injuries that I've overcome," she told *Fox4 News.*

Afterward, Madison received a big surprise gift from one of her idols. Texas Rangers' Adrian Beltre sent her an autographed baseball with the inscription: "Madison, go for it." The player's thoughtful gesture thrilled the gymnast.

Before competing in Rio, Madison made a major announcement. The teenager committed to competing at the University of California, Los Angeles on a sports scholarship. The future Bruin couldn't wait to take classes on the beautiful Westwood campus. Plus competing in NCAA gymnastics had been a dream of hers. She even learned the school's famous "eight clap" cheer in anticipation of attending her first football game.

Prior to the Olympics, Madison received some well-deserved media attention. She granted interviews to various news outlets. In nearly every article, the grateful daughter credited her parents for helping her reach her dreams.

"They will do anything to help me succeed and be happy," the appreciative daughter told *NBCOlympics.com.*

Madison always praised her coaches, Laurent and Cecile Landi, too. She trained 35 hours a day with the French-born instructors and considered them family.

"I wouldn't be the person I am today without them," she stated.

The Final Five teach President Obama a split.
The White House

The Olympic gymnastics competition began with the team event. Over two days, the American women dominated the proceedings. Aided by Madison's high-scoring uneven bars routine, Team USA won the gold medal in resounding fashion.

The competition wasn't over yet, though. Madison also qualified for the uneven bars final. She unleashed a flawless routine filled with tricky release skills and high-flying moves. The teenager's spectacular program earned her an individual silver medal.

Madison talks with her coach, Laurent Landi.
Ricardo Bufolin

"I'm very proud of what I did," she re-marked. "I'm happy."

When Madison returned home after the Olympics, her hometown swelled with pride over her accomplishments. A large group of fans greeted her at the airport with signs and hearty congratulations. The touched gymnast remem-bered how she had attended Carly Patterson and Nastia Liukin's homecomings as a young girl.

"I hope I inspired a lot of young girls," the Olympic champion remarked afterward.

It looks like she already has.

Madison smiles at the 2016 MTV VMA Awards.
Aaron J. Thornton / PR Photos

MADISON KOCIAN LINKS

INSTAGRAM
instagram.com/madison_kocian

TWITTER
twitter.com/madisonkocian

OFFICIAL WEBSITE
gym-style.com/madisonkocian

USA GYMNASTICS PROFILE
usagym.org/pages/athletes/athleteListDetail.html?id=165201

UCLA BRUINS GYMNASTICS
uclabruins.com/index.aspx?path=gym

NCAA WOMEN'S GYMNASTICS
www.ncaa.com/sports/gymnastics-women/nc

WIKIPEDIA PROFILE
en.wikipedia.org/wiki/Madison_Kocian

MADISON'S FAVORITES

WEBSITE
Pinterest

SWEET
Ice Cream

GYMNAST
Nastia Liukin

SPORTS TEAM
Texas Rangers

BASEBALL PLAYER
Adrian Beltre

COLLECTIBLE
Keychains

ACTRESS
Melissa McCarthy

SINGER
Carrie Underwood

HOBBY
Cooking

BOOK
Mind Gym

TV SHOW
The Blacklist

REALITY SERIES
America's Got Talent

FAVORITE QUOTE
Dreams don't work unless you do.

EMOJI
Kissing Face

EVENT
Uneven Bars

MADISON'S COMPETITIVE RECORD HIGHLIGHTS

2016 OLYMPICS
Team – 1
Uneven Bars – 2

2016 OLYMPIC TRIALS
Uneven Bars – 1

2016 US CHAMPIONSHIPS
Uneven Bars – 2

2015 WORLD CHAMPIONSHIPS
Team – 1
Uneven Bars – 1

2015 US CHAMPIONSHIPS
Uneven Bars – 2

2014 WORLD CHAMPIONSHIPS
Team – 1

2014 US CHAMPIONSHIPS
Uneven Bars – 2

"I'd rather have the best time of my life than win and have it be so intense that I couldn't enjoy it!"

Sports fans know Aly Raisman's story by heart. The popular gymnast won two gold medals, team and floor exercise, at the 2012 Olympics. However, she missed winning an all-around bronze medal on a controversial tiebreaker. Four years later, she returned to the Olympics hoping to win that elusive all-around medal.

On May 25, 1994, in Needham, Massachusetts, Lynn and Rick Raisman welcomed their first child into their lives. They named their newborn daughter Alexandra Rose Raisman. Over the next few years, they had three more children: Brett, Chloe, and Madison.

By the time Alexandra was a two-year-old, she became known by her nickname, Aly. The toddler took gymnastics classes with her mother in a Mommy and Me class. It came as little surprise that the youngster loved gymnastics. Her mother competed in the sport in high school.

Aly showed immense talent for gymnastics.

Eventually, the young girl transitioned from a group recreational class to individual lessons at Exxcel Gymnastics and Climbing in nearby Newton.

For many years, Aly balanced a love for gymnastics and soccer. Not only did the youngster adore both sports, but she possessed a natural talent for each one. Ultimately, though, it became increasingly difficult for the child to juggle two demanding activities. She had to choose between the two sports, and gymnastics won.

Aly has a home in Cape Cod, Massachusetts.

Aly competes on the beam.
Ricardo Bufolin

Once Aly reached level 8 gymnastics, one step separated her from the sports' top tier, elite gymnastics, where athletes competed against America's best. They also represented their country at international events, like the world championships and the Olympics. Determined to shake up her training, the adolescent switched gyms and began training with Mihai and Sylvia Brestyan at Brestyan Gymnastics. At her new training center, Aly worked alongside world champion Alicia Sacramone. She had long admired the veteran gymnast and the two developed a solid friendship. Soon Aly regarded the veteran gymnast as the older sister she never had.

Aly leaps at the 2015 World Championships.
Ricardo Bufolin

Aly plots her next move.
Ricardo Bufolin

When Alicia made the 2008 Olympic team, it inspired Aly to keep working hard so she might reach sport's biggest stage one day.

By age fourteen, Aly sat on the cusp of gymnastics greatness. The hard worker had become a familiar presence on the national stage. Although she wasn't a top gymnast yet, people regarded her as a rising star.

A typical teenager Aly sometimes relaxed in front of the television set during her free time. The fashion fanatic never missed *Gossip Girl*, loving the show's revolving closet of stylish clothes! When the gymnast needed comedic relief, she watched *Friends*, *How I Met Your Mother*, or *Modern Family*. Sometimes she reconnected with a favorite movie, like *The Last Song* or *We're the Millers*.

In 2009, Aly competed on the elite junior level. After winning the all-around bronze at nationals, she earned her first invitation to an international competition. The fifteen-year-old flew to Brazil to participate in the Junior Pan American Championships. At the significant event, she scored gold medals on team, vault, and floor exercise.

Aly poses with partner Mark Ballas.
ABC

Aly gets emotional.
Ricardo Bufolin

In 2010, Aly rose to the senior level. Her third-place finish in the all-around at nationals propelled her to a spot on the world team. She subsequently won a silver medal with her team at the 2010 World Gymnastics Championships in the Netherlands.

One year later, Aly helped capture team gold for the United States at the 2011 World Championships. She also earned her first individual world medal, a bronze on the floor exercise.

Aly in Rio
Ricardo Bufolin

In the summer of 2012, Aly competed in her first Olympic Games. She was even named captain of the U.S. women's gymnastics team, nicknamed the Fierce Five. The American squad handily captured the team title. Individually, Aly won the floor exercise event and a balance beam bronze medal. The gymnast's lone disappointment came in the all-around competition when she tied Aliya Mustafina for third place but lost the bronze medal on a tiebreaker.

In the same year, Aly also graduated from Needham High School. Although the teenager had taken online classes in later years, she still enjoyed the social aspects of school. She attended prom and her graduation ceremony.

After the 2012 London Olympics, Aly enjoyed her new celebrity life. She scored several endorsement deals and made appearances at numerous gymnastics events.

Aly felt thrilled when *Dancing with the Stars'* producers invited her to appear on their competition reality series. Paired with Mark Ballas, the talented performer danced to many different musical genres including the Rumba, Viennese

Aly: Consumate Performer
Ricardo Bufolin

Waltz, and Foxtrot. The popular gymnast eventually finished in fourth place.

Aly loved gymnastics more than anything else, though. So in spring of 2015, she made her official comeback at the City of Jesolo Trophy, where she placed third in the all-around. Five months later, the determined competitor finished third in the all-around at the 2015 USA National Gymnastics Championships and earned a return trip to worlds.

Glasgow, United Kingdom, hosted the 2015 World Gymnastics Championships. Aly helped Team USA ascend to a convincing victory over China, capturing her fourth world medal.

On her off-days, Aly treasured her free time. Sometimes she went shopping at Bloomingdale's. Other times, she relaxed at her Cape Cod home, content to lounge on the beach with family and friends. The Olympic champion also took warm baths, read books, and watched televised football games.

The following season, Aly scooped up four gold medals in two international competitions. At the 2016 USA National Gymnastics Championships in St. Louis, Missouri, she scored silver medals in three events: all-around, floor exercise, and balance beam.

In early July, Aly flew to California to compete at the 2016 Olympic Trials. She was the model of consistency in San Jose. Her performances didn't just earn her third place finishes in the all-around, balance beam, floor exercise, and vault, they also booked her a ticket to the Rio Games. Aly Raisman was returning to the Olympics!

Aly and Simone celebrate all-around medals.
Ricardo Bufolin

Aly attends the MTV VMAs
Aaron J. Thornton / PR Photos

"It doesn't even feel real," she gushed afterward. "I feel like I'm in a dream right now."

Named team captain for the second-straight Olympics, Aly used her vast experience and cool demeanor to lead the U.S. to a decisive victory in the team event. Afterward, the squad dubbed themselves the Final Five. They were the final five gymnasts under the guidance of Marta Karolyi.

Aly competed next in the individual all-around competition. Throughout the event, the focused gymnast fought hard to snag the medal that eluded her in 2012. In the end, she delivered four strong routines and won the silver medal behind Simone Biles!

"It was very special," Aly commented afterward. "It's a moment you only dream of in your wildest dreams. The crowd was screaming and yelling, and I finally did it. I was so proud."

One Olympic event remained: floor exercise. Bursting with confidence, Aly delivered a near flawless routine that showcasing her astonishing tumbling and high difficulty. Her outstanding efforts landed her the silver medal, the sixth Olympic medal of her career.

After Rio, Aly enjoyed a whirlwind media tour. Among the highlights? The Final Five appeared on *The Tonight Show Starring Jimmy Fallon*, attended the *VMAs*, and walked the red carpet at the *Country Music Awards*.

After two Olympic appearances, Aly's popularity surged to an all-time high. The Final Five captain's unflagging spirit, great work ethic, and determination had inspired a whole new generation of gymnasts who wanted to be just like Aly. And who could blame them?

ALY LINKS

TWITTER
twitter.com/aly_raisman

INSTAGRAM
instagram.com/alyraisman

FACEBOOK
facebook.com/AlyRaisman

GK ELITE'S ALY RAISMAN LEOTARDS
gkelite.com/Gymnastics-Shopby-AlyRaismanLeotards

FEAT SOCKS
featsocks.com

ALY'S FAVORITES

FOOD
Sushi & Pizza

SANDWICH
Peanut Butter & Jelly

CONDIMENT
Ketchup

TELEVISION SHOW
Gossip Girl

GYMNAST
Lilia Podkopayeva

ROLE MODEL
Taylor Swift

COLOR
Pink

EMOJI
The sassy diva

FAVORITE KARAOKE MUSIC
Celine Dion

OTHER SPORT
Soccer

ALY'S COMPETITIVE RECORD HIGHLIGHTS

2016 OLYMPIC GAMES
Floor Exercise – 2
All-Around – 2
Team – 1

2016 OLYMPIC TRIALS
All-Around – 3

2016 US CHAMPIONSHIPS
All-Around – 2

2015 WORLD CHAMPIONSHIPS
Team – 1

2015 US CHAMPIONSHIPS
All-Around – 3

2012 OLYMPIC GAMES
Floor Exercise – 1
Balance Beam – 3
Team – 1

2012 OLYMPIC TRIALS
All-Around – 3

2012 US CHAMPIONSHIPS
All-Around – 3

2011 WORLD CHAMPIONSHIPS
Team – 1
Floor Exercise – 3

2011 US CHAMPIONSHIPS
All-Around – 3

2010 WORLD CHAMPIONSHIPS
Team – 2

2010 US CHAMPIONSHIPS
All-Around – 3

FINAL FIVE TRIVIA

Which gymnast was the first to hug Zac Efron when the Final Five met him?

Laurie

Which Final Five member goes to UCLA?

Madison

Which Final Five member is nicknamed Grandma because she naps a lot?

Aly

Who is nicknamed Baby Shakira?

Laurie

Who was the first Final Five member to compete at the Rio Olympics?

Laurie

Who sometimes loves eating cereal for dinner?

Gabby

Who suggested the nickname Final Five?

Simone

Before a big event, who goes to church and lights a candle for St. Sebastian, the patron saint of sports.

Simone

Who is terrified of snakes?

Madison

Who wants Blake Lively to play her in a movie?

Aly

Whose favorite exercise machine is the elliptical?

Madison

Who loves sour pickles?

Gabby

Whose favorite television show is Pretty Little Liars?

Simone

Which Final Five Gymnast likes to knit?

Gabby

Who writes poetry in her spare time?
Laurie

Which gymnast is terrified of spiders?
Laurie

Who describes herself as clumsy?
Aly

Who wants to meet the Queen of England?
Gabby

While at the Olympics, who received a video message from Maroon 5's Adam Levine?
Laurie

Which Final Five member adores stopping at Bloomingdales?
Aly

2016 Team USA - Rio
Ricardo Bufolin

FINAL FIVE QUOTES

Aly on Gabby

"When she does anything, even a cartwheel, the girls in the stands go crazy. Your ears feel like they're gonna explode, because all the little girls love her so much,

Gabby on Madison

"Her form is just so pretty, and she's just so great to watch."

Aly on Laurie

"I forget how young Laurie is just because she's so mature. She's such a great competitor and she's so consistent. She proved that as a junior and now also as a senior."

Simone on Aly

"She's one of my role models, and I don't think there's anyone I'd rather share the podium with."

Aly on Simone

"No one goes in thinking they can beat Simone."

ABOUT THE PUBLISHER

Creative Media Publishing has produced biographies on many inspiring personalities: *Simone Biles, Nadia Comaneci, Clayton Kershaw, Mike Trout, Yuna Kim, Shawn Johnson, Nastia Liukin, The Fierce Five, Gabby Douglas, Sutton Foster, Kelly Clarkson, Idina Menzel, Missy Franklin* and more. They've published two award-winning Young Adult novels, *Cutters Don't Cry* (Moonbeam Children's Book Award) and *Kaylee: The "What If?" Game* (Children's Literary Classic Awards). They have also produced a line of popular children's book series, including *The Creeper and the Cat, Future Presidents Club, Princess Dessabelle* and *Quinn: The Ballerina*.

www.CreativeMedia.net
@CMIPublishing

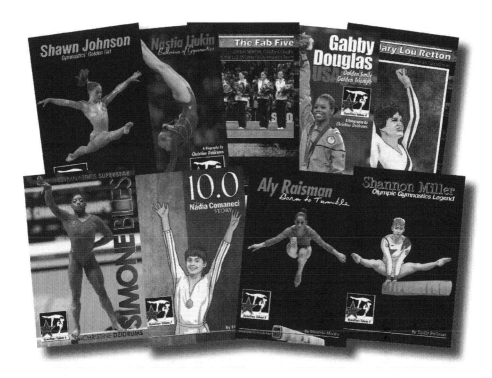

Now sports fans can learn about gymnastics' greatest stars! Americans **Shawn Johnson** and **Nastia Liukin** became the darlings of the 2008 Beijing Olympics when the fearless gymnasts collected 9 medals between them. Four years later at the 2012 London Olympics, America's **Fab Five** claimed gold in the team competition. A few days later, **Gabby Douglas** added another gold medal to her collection when she became the fourth American woman in history to win the Olympic all-around title. The *GymnStars* series reveals these gymnasts' long, arduous path to Olympic glory. *Gabby Douglas: Golden Smile, Golden Triumph* received a **2012 Moonbeam Children's Book Award**.

At the 2010 Vancouver Olympics, tragic circumstances thrust **Joannie Rochette** into the spotlight when her mother died two days before the ladies short program. Joannie then captured hearts everywhere by courageously skating two moving programs to win the Olympic bronze medal.
Joannie Rochette: Canadian Ice Princess profiles the popular figure skater's moving journey.

Meet figure skating's biggest star: **Yuna Kim**. The Korean trailblazer produced two legendary performances at the 2010 Vancouver Olympic Games to win the gold medal. *Yuna Kim: Ice Queen* uncovers the compelling story of how the beloved figure skater overcame poor training conditions, various injuries and numerous other obstacles to become world and Olympic champion.

Our *YNot Girl* series chronicles the lives and careers of the world's most famous role models. *Jennie Finch: Softball Superstar* details the California native's journey from a shy youngster to softball's most famous face. In *Kelly Clarkson: Behind Her Hazel Eyes*, young readers will find inspiration reading about the superstar's rise from a broke waitress with big dreams to becoming one of the recording industry's top musical acts. *Missy Franklin: Swimming Sensation* narrates the Colorado native's transformation from a talented swimming toddler to queen of the pool.

Theater fans first fell for **Sutton Foster** in her triumphant turn as *Thoroughly Modern Millie*. Since then the triple threat has charmed Broadway audiences by playing a writer, a princess, a movie star, a nightclub singer, and a Transylvania farm girl. Now the two-time Tony winner is conquering television in the acclaimed series *Bunheads*. A children's biography, ***Sutton Foster: Broadway Sweetheart, TV Bunhead*** details the role model's rise from a tiny ballerina to the toast of Broadway and Hollywood.

Idina Menzel's career has been "Defying Gravity" for years! With starring roles in *Wicked* and *Rent*, the Tony-winner is one of theater's most beloved performers. The powerful vocalist has also branched out in other mediums. She has filmed a recurring role on television's smash hit *Glee* and lent her talents to the Disney films, *Enchanted* and *Frozen*. A children's biography, ***Idina Menzel: Broadway Superstar*** narrates the actress' rise to fame from a Long Island wedding singer to overnight success!

Twelve-year-old Emylee Markette has felt invisible her entire life. Then one fateful afternoon, three beautiful sisters arrive in her sleepy New England town and instantly become the most popular girls at Forest Springs Middle School. To everyone's surprise, the Fay sisters befriend Emylee and welcome her into their close-knit circle. Before long, the shy loner finds herself running with the cool crowd, joining the track team and even becoming friends with her lifelong crush.

Through it all, though, Emylee's weighed down by nagging suspicions. Why were the Fay sisters so anxious to befriend her? How do they know some of her inner thoughts? What do they truly want from her?

When Emylee eventually discovers that her new friends are secretly fairies, she finds her life turned upside down yet again and must make some life-changing decisions.

Fair Youth: Emylee of Forest Springs marks the first volume in an exciting new book series.

Ashley Moore wants to know why there's never been a girl president. Before long the inspired six-year-old creates a special, girls-only club - the **Future Presidents Club**. Meet five enthusiastic young girls who are ready to change the world. *Future Presidents Club: Girls Rule* is the first book in a series about girls making a difference!

Meet **Princess Dessabelle**, a spoiled, lonely princess with a quick temper.

In ***Princess Dessabelle Makes a Friend***, the lonely youngster discovers the meaning of true friendship. ***Princess Dessabelle: Tennis Star*** finds the pampered girl learning the importance of good sportsmanship.

Quinn the Ballerina can hardly believe it's finally performance day. She's playing her first principal role in a production of *The Sleeping Beauty*.

Yet, Quinn is also nervous. Can she really dance the challenging steps? Will people believe her as a cursed princess caught in a 100-year spell?

Join Quinn as she transforms into Princess Aurora in an exciting retelling of Tchaikovsky's *The Sleeping Beauty*. Now you can relive, or experience for the first time, one of ballet's most acclaimed works as interpreted by a 9 year old.

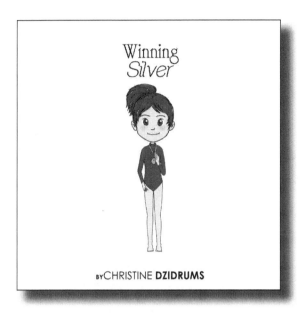

Winning
Silver

ʙʏCHRISTINE **DZIDRUMS**

What happens when Elise delivers perfect routines but doesn't win? Can the disappointed gymnast accept the silver medal when she dreamed only of gold?

Filled with adorable illustrations and armed with straightforward storytelling, *Winning Silver* stresses the importance of good sportsmanship. Anyone who has ever felt gutted by a competitive result will relate to Elise's initial disappointment over not getting the result she expected.

From the popular new series, ***Classical Reboots,*** *Rapunzel* updates the **Brothers Grimm** fairy tale with hilarious and heartbreaking results.

Rapunzel has been locked in her adoptive mother's attic for years. Just as the despondent teenager abandons hope of escaping her private prison, a mysterious tablet computer appears. Before long, Rapunzel's quirky fairy godmother, Aiko, has the conflicted young girl questioning her place in the world.

Cutters Don't Cry

2010 Moonbeam Children's Book Award Winner! In a series of raw journal entries written to her absentee father, a teenager chronicles her penchant for self-harm, a serious struggle with depression and an inability to vocally express her feelings.

Kaylee: The 'What If?' Game

"I play the 'What If?'" game all the time. It's a cruel, wicked game."

When free spirit Kaylee suffers a devastating loss, her personality turns dark as she struggles with depression and un-resolved anger. Can Kaylee repair her broken spirit, or will she remain a changed person?

17082437R00064

Made in the USA
Middletown, DE
26 November 2018